The Summer Of
My Content

The Summer Of My Content

Glenn & Sue Hawks
119 Don Felipe Way
Ojai, Calif 93023

Elaine Cannon

Published by
Deseret Book Company
Salt Lake City, Utah
1976

© 1976 by
Deseret Book Company
All Rights Reserved
ISBN 0-87747-585-7
Library of Congress Catalog Card No. 76-292
Printed in the United States of America

Contents

Chapter One

The Hill

*T*here is in summer a continuum imperceptibly marking the shift from year to year, age to age, wisdom to wisdom. Summer is the only time enough to learn all the things that can't be taught in the classroom.

When as an infant we moved to 391 Wall Street on Capitol Hill, The Hill was set apart by the natural boundaries of Ensign Peak, City Creek Canyon, and Main Street sloping into town. Our houses clustered about the massive Utah State Capitol, making our neighborhood unique, tight knit, and highly motivating.

It was before land developers, so the houses on the Hill were individual—like the people inside. The split shake shingle with its brooding overhangs and the simple facsimile of a French chateau mingled comfortably with the red brick bungalow, the Christmas-card-cottage, and the pioneer cabin remodeled for another generation's needs. The only apartment was a haphazard affair constructed before building restrictions, but it broadened our experience with a transient element that some grownups resisted.

The people on the Hill were largely Mormon. Some conformed to strict standards. Some did not. But they all showed up for every groundbreaking, funeral, three-act play, and missionary farewell on the schedule at the meetinghouse.

Living on the Hill was a child's paradise where summer was a rare blend of the mysteries of the wilderness and sophistications of a capital city. We scaled peaks and the rickety ladder to the Capitol dome in equal excitement. We became conscious of flag ceremonies and the poignancy of "Taps" at sunset long before we could tie our own sneakers. We explored caves one day and the silent chambers of the Senate the next. We became friends with the Governor and the gardener alike. We hounded the state chemist, keeper of countless glass tubes, but we learned more about sanitation by studiously avoiding wading in City Creek. Signs posted everwhere along its winding route reminded that this was the water we drank and nobody's feet were declared clean enough!

We were taught early that for us meadowlarks warbled "Salt Lake City is a pretty little place" and that if worse came to worst, we, like the pioneers who settled this valley, could exist on the roots of the sego lilies dotting the brown slopes behind the Capitol.

Summers on Capitol Hill held special compensation for a city child. Though we didn't have the company of cows, horses, and roosters to crow in the dawn, we did have the Capitol lions. These great creatures that guarded the east and west entrances to the edifice were frankly considered our private property.

How we would clamor over those lions, stretching ourselves cool over the bony backs. We'd examine the haunches, the tails, the claws. We'd finger the eyes and rule the world from our perch behind the great mane. Though they were just cast cement, it was only on our

2

truly brave days that we dared edge our way up front to scrunch under the jaws and sit in the circle of the forelegs. Sometimes we'd feast on our supply of stale Easter eggs kept hidden in a secret place for emergencies.

When we wearied of lions, we'd descend upon the confines of the Capitol itself. First we'd prowl the dark ground level with case after case of stuffed buffalo and coyotes, of prize-winning Utah grains, and produce displayed in enormous fancy glass jars that enhanced the appearance of the product considerably but never made us hungry.

Or we'd do a few somersaults on the brass railings guarding the giant black block of Utah bituminous coal, before brushing past the politicians to the sacred floors above. Visitors were awe-struck at the beauty of this building built in the days of early western settlements. We'd sit for hours studying the enormous murals at each end, depicting such heritage as was ours. The vast dome itself, painted with fleecy clouds, rivaled the sky for inspiration. The halls, the balconies, the balustrades with their cold iron eagles offered endless settings for fantasies that filled our young souls between Memorial and Labor days. Endless settings, inside and outside, all summer long. We knew it all so well!

We followed the guided tours so many times we could give the lectures ourselves by the time we turned ten. We knew how much gold leaf bathed the ornate walls of the formal reception room, and we were hard pressed sometimes to not jump the gun on the tour guide. And if he forgot, we were quick to point out the butterfly formed by the veining in one of the giant marble columns. Oh, those columns! They were so huge we could hug only half and a child was well hidden at game.

Before heading for home, we would beg cigar boxes from the newsstand and make doll beds to drag around behind us on a long string. The stand man, in his funny red

fez, would patiently poke a hole in the end of the box with
his ice pick and supply us with great lengths of string.
Once home, I had to cover any trace of tobacco language on
the box with magazine pictures or doilies, or abandon the
homemade doll bed because Mother was adamant about
our avoiding the very appearance of evil.

Sometimes in summer my family would picnic under
the catalpa trees shading the Capitol's western slopes.
We'd look out over the old section of Salt Lake City with
its quaint-gabled, adobe brick houses and the beloved
black Tabernacle, fat and squat like a potato bug com-
manding its own place in the shadow of the pristine spires
of the Holy House of the Lord (as we then called the temple
on Temple Square). We took turns pointing out the kinds
of trees and spelling the names and chorusing together at
last that the first trees were carried across the plains to
green-up the Salt Desert land our city had sprung from.
Cottonwoods for shade, poplars to break the wind, mountain elm because they grew so fast.

Mother would tell us stories about her pioneer heritage so we would know we had "roots" until Daddy, bereft
of ancestors who had crossed the plains, brought us back to
reality with ambitious plans for the Capitol Hill Improvement League, he being its founder and president.

"Capitol Hill Improvement League," I invariably
murmured to myself. How could this area be *improved*?
Why the Capitol, the grounds, the secret places and public
face of it all proved our purposeful playground summer
after summer. The hills and houses surrounding us were
the kingdom of our delight and seat of our best learnings.
The people loved life and worked hard. Like Whitman's
child that went forth, these things and these places and the
people who happened there in that time, these became part
of me in the stretching cycles of summer.

Chapter Two

In The Season Thereof

The summer we painted the oleander was the beginning of a lifelong attitude about appropriateness. One doesn't gild the lily. One doesn't tamper with natural beauty.

An oleander in Utah was something of a novelty in those days. Ours was the family treasure. Daddy had invested something of himself in that plant. Some years before, he had packed it in soggy cotton and brought it on the long trip from California to his mother in Salt Lake City. When Grandmother died, it was ours and the more valuable because it had been hers. It was nurtured, protected. Each winter, ceremoniously, it was swathed in burlap and hauled into the garage. Each time we climbed into the Studebaker it was at the command, "Don't crush the oleander." Each summer it was brought forth to be hosed down, pot-painted, and put in place by the porch. Then at last profuse blooms rewarded everyone.

On this particular day I was suffering—at age three—the tortures of rejection. There was some painting going on at our house and I had been programmed out. When the supplies were left unguarded, I sought to beautify the oleander. What sport!

What a sense of power I felt changing the look of that shrub with each flamboyant slap of the brush until the shrieks of my parents awakened me to my mischief. It was not beautiful at all. It was ruined, its pitiful petals sticking together in extravagant blueness.

"One cannot improve on God," Daddy declared emphatically, shaking me soundly.

The oleander died, of course, but Daddy's counsel lives in me yet. A chair can be repainted to cover past damage, but a living, growing thing can be spoiled forever through witless tampering. And that goes for people as well as plants.

It was Daddy who would take my hand each spring and say, "Come along. It's time to see if there is a violet brave enough to weather the storms. Should we go see if summer is coming after all?" Then we'd gently brush aside sodden, left-over leaves in a sunny corner and always there would be a violet. Daddy was a wonder to me. He knew just when to look.

Of course, I grew up loving earth's green things and in the season thereof they were plentiful and varied to us on the Hill because of the Capitol's spectacular offerings.

The formal gardens south of the Capitol fascinated me. There were trimmed hedges that spelled "Utah" and exotic blooms the home gardener could never afford. The gentle slopes so perfect for sleigh riding, Easter egg rolls, or somersaults in season were lined with cherry trees imported from distant Japan. All these were cared for by a gifted man who suffered from arthritis. We used to watch him wince when he stooped to cup new pansy plants into damp earth beds. He hobbled home from work past our house late each day, each step a new agony. No one questioned why he didn't change jobs. He was lucky to have one. But we were careful not to trample his gardens in thoughtless summer games.

One day I sat guarding our lemonade stand while Marilyn went for more ice chips. The street car would be along soon, and we almost always got some customers at this stop if there were ice chips in clean tin cups for the drink. I passed the time watching the gardener. He looked so hot, even from where I sat, and he moved like he hurt more than usual. Oh, I felt so sorry for him! Then I had a great idea. I'd treat him to some of our lemonade—free. It wasn't very cold but it was wet, and he'd know somebody cared about him. For safekeeping, I pocketed the pennies we'd taken in and stored in Mother's celluloid hair receiver Then I crossed the street with the cup of lemonade.

"Well, thank you," he said, sipping it carefully. "You've added just enough sugar."

Some people downed their drinks in one gulp, so of course they couldn't tell if our mix was good or not. The gardener tasted it. He knew. Just as he knew which plants had the softest leaves and that my eyes were brown and not blue. He finished drinking and said that since I had done him such a kind favor, he was going to do one for me—he was going to show me a kind of miracle. We walked over to the colorful bed of coleus plants, all dark red and green trimmed and velvety. He troweled one up and put it into my hands after interlocking my fingers so the soil wouldn't spill off the roots. I was to pot it, water it just so, and place it in a sunny window where I could watch "the miracle."

He took one ruffled leaf gently and, lifting it with his knobby fingers, said, "The coleus plant will lean to light. Turn your plant every two or three days and the leaves will turn right around again and lean to the light. Try it, Elaine. You'll see the miracle. And maybe it's something you'd like to do with your life."

No wonder we held him and his handiwork in a kind of reverence.

9

Chapter Three

Heaven's Reach

*T*he summer of sacrifice was the year everyone helped build the new stone chapel with contributions of labor or hard cash.

We had been meeting in the converted carriage house behind the McCune mansion, and the groundbreaking for our building was a celebration. So was the day the trucks dumped their loads of fieldstone on the site. We children had helped pay for those stones (bricks were too costly) by saving pennies in peanut butter jars, peddling needles and shoe laces door to door, or selling lemonade at the streetcar stops with the proceeds going for the cause. Edgar worked up a deal with the publishers of *Liberty* magazine and sold subscriptions. Mother was so impressed with his enterprising spirit that she signed up for two years. The sacrifice part came when someone suggested that instead of going downtown to the Saturday movie matinee, the children were to contribute their show money for stones.

Naturally, we were very interested in this project and hung around the church lot across from the Capitol the better part of one summer.

The old stonemason had set up shop on the grounds and, being "hired" help from off the Hill, he was a unique being. He wore clothes that matched his scarred, stained hands which reflected years at his trade. He only shaved for Sunday. In utter fascination, we watched the daily growth darken on his jawline and under his sharp nose. He didn't pay much attention to us children, but his young apprentice counted anything that breathed as his personal audience. The stonemason's hands were swift and sure, and it seemed he seldom rested from his labors. The apprentice, on the other hand, did a lot of leaning. Oh, he'd mix a little mortar or wheel a barrow full of stones to the workbench now and then, but mostly he just leaned, posturing and turning his bare, bronze body this way and that in the sun before our dazzled eyes.

The stonemason seldom spoke. The brash young apprentice knew all the filthy words to say and said them. Frequently. One day he was being especially coarse when the old man "finally got his dander up," as Mother would say when her temper flared. He raised his voice and announced solemnly: "No point in teaching these kids the ugly things when there are so many pretty things to talk about." And with a whap of his tool, the stonemason split a dull gray stone into colorful, shimmering halves ready to be mortared into walls. There was a sermon in those stones.

For me, from that day forward, the Capitol Hill Ward rose as a monument to the fact that you can't tell the inside of a thing by its covering—even with people.

This can be true of books too, I discovered in later years. Some of the fanciest bindings housed only trash. Some of the scroungiest-looking books spilled forth rare beauty, inspiration, and challenge.

For instance, one day in my early teens a boy slipped me a coverless collection of English verse with pages torn, worn, and soiled, but it changed my life. This passage was marked: "Ah, but a man's reach should exceed his grasp, or what's a heaven for?"

So wrote Browning decades before I read it fresh that day and took it personally, appropriate to my season of self-discovery, of hopeful idealism and firming philosophy. And I might never have reached if I'd been stopped by the cover.

That is another blessed blessing of summer—time enough to read and to know what you've read. I'd pick a few Italian plums from our tree and rub off the powdery white until the dark skins glistened red-purple. Then I'd retreat to the Capitol slope and read in the cool of sprinkler spray splashing off tree trunks, soon oblivious to the ka-chugging sound the rain-bird made.

In my summers I had romped through the Mark Tidd books, the Anne of Green Gables series, and plowed through a Tarzan book or two just to please my brother. I had discovered the Lloyd C. Douglas books and dreamed of my own magnificent obsession. And I had fallen down Alice's rabbit hole and climbed Heidi's Alp seven or eight times by the summer I learned of Heaven's Reach and the truth, one more time, about covers.

Worn leather volumes containing Shakespeare, Wordsworth, Longfellow, and Chaucer were passed into my hands by this boy who understood the grasp-and-reach theory. The public library provided me with ugly, stiff, practical new bindings of Dickens and Robert Louis Stevenson and Emerson's Essay on Friendship with the library number perforated across random pages. Then came the sharing of a simple maroon book called *Larry* after the remarkable young man whose letters and journal entries and notes to Girl, his girl, were collected therein. We read that, and when he died in the end, almost before he had really lived, we wept.

I loved all these books unabashedly.

This boy and I couldn't understand everything we read, but it was so exhilarating trying to understand that it was like coming in with the tide! Stretching our minds in the reading and then struggling to say it back in our own words to each other kept our relationship going one swift summer and was the basis for a lifelong friendship.

We'd read and we'd walk and we'd sit on the curb and we'd talk. The reading, the matching of the masters against our Master, was sacred and stimulating business and fodder for the fires of friendship.

And I went through all that soul-soaring and nobody in my family noticed what had happened to me. I was different inside but they went on treating me in the same old way around the house, just as my familiar drab "cover" dictated.

It was frustrating to me and I tried to tell Mother about it one night. We sat on the porch in the dark, conscious of the cool cement beneath us. Somewhere "Harbor Lights" was being played. Somewhere a baby cried and the Barton boy disturbed the night peace practicing his trumpet. Mother was so quiet when I stopped talking that I thought she didn't understand.

Then she said, "Well, I've always heard that the face you have when you are forty is exactly what you deserve! A person's cover comes quietly, Elaine, matching character only at the end, I believe. That's why it can be so cruel to judge others when you only see the outside of them."

Mother understood and I'm beginning to.

Chapter Four

What Money Can't Buy

The mother of a dear friend of mine used to say to us, "Summer is when you can enjoy all the things money can't buy." And how right she was. Who can match with dollars the unbroken hours with a good book or getting into a long-awaited project or simply wallowing in fragrant clover patches or watching the miracle of blossoms become peaches? And what of playing Kick-the-Can and Run, Sheepie, Run until dusk was done behind Antelope Island?

The summer we first played a game we called "Stink" on the Capitol plaza was the summer we became conscious of some of life's ugliness. Old Mr. Wright came to visit his sister that year and each night he wavered past our game. Each day we would secretly stare at the different state of him. It was a frightening novelty in our sheltered Mormon neighborhood. I'm not sure now whether we played that game because it was fun or so we could get another look at a drunk man. "Inebriated," Mother put it, and said we were not to stare.

One night Mr. Wright's stumble flattened him. We stopped the game to laugh—until he didn't get up. Then two of the boys—suddenly men—ran to help. The rest of us strained to see, at once curious and repelled. His nose was bleeding all over him and his legs buckled repeatedly as the boys wrestled with him. As they half-dragged, half-carried him to his door, a wonderful awareness came over me. The Word of Wisdom was true! Youth and cleanness, uprightness and self-control were to be desired. Drink wasn't very funny after all. It turned a man into something less, and I vowed then and there never to taste a drop.

One summer the goal was jumping—high jumping, rope jumping, broad jumping, pole vaulting. We'd spend hours with a bamboo pole until it frayed at the bottom from being rammed into the summer-crusted soil. We'd use grass cuttings to land on and another pole propped between Wood's back fence and our chickenwire grape arbor as the riser.

But down the street was where the summer jumping was best. Aunt Effie and Aunt Cora lived in twin yellow brick houses at the top of Wall Street's hill. They commanded a view of the lake, the oil works, Warm Springs, and the road to Lagoon. From the upstairs back bedroom, you had the best view in town of the summer sunsets made firelike in the salt prismed rays off the lake, of the fireworks on the Fourth from the fairgrounds on Ninth West, and you could watch the planes lift and land from the black strip on the salt flats.

Inside, you couldn't tell those houses apart. The same people breezed in and out of kitchens and cupboards in both places with equal ease. Both had good things going, like the huge kettle with the makings for Mrs. B's tutti-fruiti ice cream waiting for one of the older boys to come home and turn the hand freezer. And like the tummy-growling aroma of sweet basil and beef bones in the soup pot on the stove, fat raisin-filled cookies cooling on the sill, or potawatami jam made from the fruit of the huge old plum tree between the houses, getting its last skim before sealing. Sometimes somebody would silence us with a chomp of the paraffin wax that we'd flavor with a piece of nasturtium leaf.

Outside, the houses had one big difference. Aunt Cora's had a high balcony at the end of its second-floor hall. The one who could climb the bricks to the balcony and jump from there to the lawn below without spraining an ankle, breaking a leg, or crying was declared champion— champions being very important people in those days of beginning professional athletics and dance marathons. We spent more time calculating the jumps than jumping just because it was fun being around there. Aunt Cora and Aunt Effie were real live polygamist wives left over from the Manifesto. They were old and spoke of the past in soft, sweet tones as if they were still in the middle of it. They reminded me of a painting I'd seen at the Capitol, beautiful in clean aprons with enormous pockets over long skirts and black stockings. I always got the feeling they were very very good and had nothing in this world to worry about.

Married children and their families peopled those homes now, too, because times were hard, but the all-in-one-family feeling persisted down the generations in an aura of love seldom equaled in the "regular" homes we frequented. Daddy said he guessed that maybe everyone tried so hard in the beginning long ago that now graciousness was not only a habit, it was their way of life.

But not everyone knew about graciousness.

It was almost the end of July when a man up the street decided the youth of the neighborhood needed some place to play. In a great flurry of pipes, chains, and sand, the vacant lot next to his house took on the look of a playground. We watched the progress with delight until it was finished at last. Not only had this man engineered this project, but now we discovered he was also self-appointed king, guard, and referee. We were not to use the equipment unless he was there. We were not to race freely to see who could get to the stairs of the tall slide first. We were not to blithely catch a swing.

We were assigned and policed "for our own good."

But with our right to choose threatened, the fun was gone. Soon the chute only shaded sleeping dogs, the swings hung still, the monkey bars were a hollow marking against the summer sky.

That summer we worked hard at proving we didn't need the playground. Agency was now very valuable to us, so everyone made a great production about deciding things like whether we'd paint Sister Hunter's fence while she told us about her spiritual experiences, play "Bat" in the cool comfort of the Capitol, or climb on those massive Lions at the gates.

On days when a hunger for real live creatures took precedence over pounding hearts, we'd dare ourselves to go spy on the neighborhood "witch." Actually, she wasn't "right in her head," according to our parents, and therefore the city let her have a few farm animals to keep her content.

The place was a mess and like nothing you'd care to hear described, but it was alive with animals novel to us. A purebred boxer plus a lamb, twelve cats, a goat, and a flock of ducks were her "children." They lived in her house and she called each one by name. We were terrified of her but the animals were not. They answered her call, nuzzled her legs, and ate from her hand—all living in peace.

Although we children were about the only humans to venture near her, she rarely paid any attention to us—only if we pestered the creatures, and then we'd be whisked out with a cane. But mostly we'd sneak around watching her chatter with the animals until we began to feel like eavesdroppers. Sometimes we would taunt her with a sing-song "Crazy witch! Crazy witch! Sews her clothes without a stitch." Then we'd scramble over the splintery fence, hands slivery, necks sweaty and prickly, hearts thumping in delicious terror.

Once when we were there, Henrietta the duck wandered out into the path of the ice wagon. This poor old lady didn't seem crazy to me then as she crooned a kind of lullaby, cradling that duck until long after it died.

I went home that day feeling confused, my cheeks hot with shame. I, who had struggled to get a trained dog to answer my call, finally realized that her secret wasn't sorcery—it was love.

And that's something money can't buy.

Chapter Five

Minutia

*S*ummers I spent a lot of time sitting on the curb. Curbs were a fine new mark of our civilization and therefore an attraction. "Built-in benches for babes" was the way Daddy teased us, but he'd been instrumental in getting them there, so we didn't mind.

We considered curbs our private property and therefore felt perfectly safe sitting there watching the world go by. I sat on the curb to wait for Larona to get home from kindergarten, to watch Brent work on his old model T, to count cars in a funeral procession, or to watch the couples court by the pine trees on the Capitol grounds. I sat on the curb to float boats in the gutter, so clean in those days with mountain water forever running away. We'd squat to tie a shoe lace or carefully fold down our long lisle stockings on the first warm day of the season.

It was a daily plan for Betty and me to meet halfway at the church on the corner. We sat there for nearly seventeen summers—right on up through high school—surveying the scene or solving the problems of life. The view of the Capitol was perfect. We watched dignitaries come and the wonderfully intricate wrought iron, fencing the state's property, go. We watched people take their driving license tests around the newly created parking lot. Demonstrating parallel parking skill was the tough one for most folks, and we sat shivering in delicious agony about whether we'd pass or not when our turn came—if ever!

You could see all kinds of things from a curb and nobody paid you any mind. It was as if you were part of the scenery. We used to watch Mrs. Widley hang up her wash. Her clothesline was in plain sight of the street. She had much more formal education than other women on the Hill and didn't make a fetish of getting her clothes out first Monday morning. But she did have a fascinating, undeviating system for setting out the week's laundry when she got around to it.

She hung from the inside lines and worked out. She must have organized everything in the house, because by the time she was finished, the whole thing was shielded by sheets. Mother said the breezes couldn't blow through and fluff things up that way. Every woman had to defend her own habits, I guess. My own opinion was it was too bad to hide all those clothes because they looked so nice the way she did it.

Towels were flipped and folded lengthwise and pinned neatly according to size, color, and use (bathroom, company best, and kitchen) with the washcloths and dishrags separating each kind. Stockings were matched and hung all of a size together in a section of line. Coverall legs were pinned even to the line—three pins per leg—not folded over to leave an ugly bend in the bottom. She'd stretch and pull the cotton T shirts back into shape and alternate them with the shorts. When they came down, a top and bottom were folded up neatly together! Petticoats and pantywaists were carefully covered with aprons, but the union suits dangled freely from the shoulders to march crazily along the line—dancing in whatever wind—like an army having underwear inspection.

Taking down was done according to a system, too. All the kitchen things were piled together; all the things to be mended and all the starched goods had their stacks. Her work was half done, her ironing greatly lessened with this procedure. We never tired of watching the ritual and I benefited greatly from such instruction when I became a bride, because it all came back to me the day I did my first wash.

On the Twenty-fourth of July holiday, we'd shift our curb sitting to the south edge of the Hill. We'd plop down on the curb for a bird's-eye view of the Pioneer Day Parade meandering down Main Street. Those wonderfully wide streets Brigham Young had insisted upon allowed all kinds of remarkable band formations and posse performances. And there was plenty of room for a full review.

From where we sat, we could watch the exciting confusion of the gathering and the maneuvering of un-wieldy floats between the Hotel Utah and the temple, where the line-up took place. The horses reared under rein and people crossed and recrossed the street in an endless parade of their own. Nothing stayed put. But then, one by one, the units started past the Brigham Young monument in a miracle of elegant orderliness for public approval and a powerful reminder of their heritage.

I never saw a prettier parade than one back in the twenties when I was a very little girl. Maybe another one has never equaled it because I grew older and the aura of childhood wonder was outlived by other excitements. But maybe it was because I was in it.

Instead of curb sitting, this time the family walked on down the Hill together. A close-up seemed important this time. Mom and the others positioned themselves in front of the old Constitution Building. She liked facing the unique store front of Zion's Cooperative Mercantile In-stitution, and the children could buy refreshment from the heat in the Grabeteria nearby, where Daddy often ate lunch.

I bounced beside Daddy to the Primary Children's Hospital just west of Main across from the north gate of Temple Square. I was to ride on their float. I was in a long white nightgown and had a new ribbon to band over my bangs. My heart was pounding with unfamiliar self-importance. And there it was—the most beautiful of floats awaiting the arrival of its queen. My throne, I soon discovered, was a hospital bed. Well, I could handle that! But what did disturb me was the lady in charge. Fortunately I can't remember who she was, only how she was. I silently figured I never wanted to be "in charge" of anything if that's how it made you be. Her first words when she saw me were, "Good grief! We chose her because she was so skinny she looked sick. Take off that hair ribbon!"

And she yanked it off my head and then began frantically pounding my face with powder—all of my face, eyes, nose, mouth, and even my bangs.

So they chose me because I looked sick. Daddy's tender heart thumped for mine and when the make-up was finished, he asked if I might be taken in to say goodbye to the children in the hospital. Personally I didn't want anybody seeing me like this. If they thought I looked sick before—

But Daddy was wisely unwavering. We went in and the nurse told the children I was to represent them on their float. And then, oh then, what a time it turned out to be. They clapped and they shouted. They thumped their crutches and rocked their wheelchairs.

Hoorah! For *me*!

I was overwhelmed. Humbled. And, oh mercy, I nearly cried right there in front of everybody. It was only the thought of a repeat on the powdering that helped me hold back the tears.

Then they put me high on the float, in the bed,

covered up. My nightgown didn't show. My hair ribbon was gone. My face was an unrecognizable mess. But as we moved out onto Main Street I felt a small surge of usefulness swell deep inside of me as if I had taken all of their terrible suffering onto my skinny shoulders.

And all I had to do was look sick!

All the particulars of past scenes and glad scenes, all the minutia of delight upon delight can never equal the joy of that parade.

Chapter Six

Unto Others

*S*ummer and winter alike, vacations and holidays not-withstanding, our whole family went to church—everybody, everytime. Sometimes it was really interesting, especially when Brother and Sister Rawson performed their duet: he played the harmonica and she whistled. They were genial people who cooked the church suppers or provided entertainment as needed. They each had a huge stomach and I always wondered how they dared to stand up in public like that with so much of themselves sticking out. But they put on a good act and gave a whole new sound to the hymns. Sometimes Jessie Evans sang "He that Hath Clean Hands" in a way that made me look at mine a second time.

The only way you escaped from the tortures of a boring speaker on a hot summer night was to convince your mother you needed the restroom and couldn't wait until you got home. A speaker knew how well he was doing by the number of children filing out.

One July night we were hearing about the pioneers again, and the speaker was as dry as the plains our ancestors had crossed. People waved their fans vigorously in a valiant effort to stay awake. I'd already been out, so I was trying to entertain myself by looking at the people. Sometimes that was more fun than anything. Like old Sister Huebner and her fan. Most of us used the cardboard kind passed out to us at the door. There was advertising on the back, like "Is Your Life Insurance Beneficial" with an enormous question mark curling around the slogan. But Mrs. Huebner had one made out of cut ivory that collapsed and expanded from a base with a silk tassle dangling. She had a tricky way of using it, too. She'd fan on the downswing, fold up the fan on the upswing, fan on the downswing, fold up on the upswing. About the fifth or sixth sequence her head would begin to nod and she would hit her nose. My brother Lowell and I were betting hairpins from Mother's purse on which stroke she would hit her nose, when suddenly her fan got caught in her nostril! There simply was no stopping our giggles. We stuffed our mouths with handkerchiefs. We hid our red faces in the hymnbook. We suffered Mother to clap her hands over our eyes so we couldn't look at each other and burst out laughing again. But we couldn't stop. It was a marvelous relief to be whisked from the church at last. Disgrace may have been ours for the moment, but so was freedom.

That night, before bed, Mother took us into the dining room to talk to us about Behavior Unto Others. I remember best the part about treating other people as you'd like to be treated, especially when they were trying their best. That's when Heavenly Father smiled upon you, she explained, when you were nice to someone even when you didn't feel like it. Then she kissed us anyway.

One summer Sunday, my friend Vic showed up at our house a while before church and said bread was needed for the sacrament. Mother quickly wrapped two loaves of fresh-from-the-oven bread. Because it was for the sacrament, none of us grumbled much, until later when some-

30

thing very peculiar happened at the meeting. There was a bit of jostling in our aisle by a couple of the deacons, but finally Vic lost the scuffle and had to serve our family the tray of bread bits. Instead of Mother's, it was sticky bakery bread, and as Mother caught his eye, Vic went scarlet. After the meeting Mother approached him. Before she could say anything, Vic went through the agonies, protestations, and explanations that guilt generates. When it was her turn to talk, she merely said, "Vic, how would you like to come over and wash my bread pans next time?" Relief, repentance, and the hope of some restitution for the blasphemy of using the sacrament as an excuse for a home-made bread "bust" out in the field, flooded his face. When he finished the job, a day or so later, I noticed Mother gave him two of the crusty ends of new bread.

Summer wasn't going to be ruined after all.

It was our custom to kneel in family prayer. In winter families were secreted together inside with sounds of the stoker rattling the coal furnace in the basement and the smell of dinner still fragrant. Prayer didn't seem an interruption then. It was a cozy part of the season. Somebody was always sick, too, and blessings were a valid need.

But in summer, when light still lingered and dogs and children romped in noisy delight on our front lawn, it was different. The voices of the neighborhood kids were a painful distraction, wafting in and out of my consciousness like the furls of a flag in a soft wind, revealing only part of the pattern with each breeze. I'd strain to hear who was already out, what they were saying, which game they were playing while we were still praying. I longed to fly free into the evening cooled by canyon breezes and leave my miserable body there, prostrate over the chair.

We would kneel in the dining room, scene of all formal moments in our family life, each child to a chair so there was less jostling during the prayer. I kept my eyes open until the last moment before the prayer started, studying the hardwood floor marred by an ink spot Junior had made doing his homework, its irregular shape forever on the floor, forever in my mind.

When Daddy prayed it was always longer. He blessed everyone up and down the block by name. Often I couldn't follow what he said because the words were unfamiliar and the style unlike our comfortable conversations. He'd say things like, "Father, we thank thee that all is in accord and that the personnel of this family is complete and accounted for."

Once I visited his office and heard him dictate letters while I waited for a ride up the hot hill. That was it! His prayers were like he was giving dictation. That night when he prayed, I risked the wrath of heaven and sneaked a look at Daddy's face. I was startled. He was weeping! The language he spoke was formal like his letters to important people, but the tears running down his cheeks spoke volumes about the tenderness in his heart.

Daddy loved Heavenly Father so much he spoke to him in the best language he knew. It was that experience that made me restless with my habitual bedtime routine "Now I lay me down to sleep. . ." That summer I ventured a prayer from my heart in my own language instead of reciting something memorized in somebody else's.

Across the street and half down the block was a house with a huge front porch. That porch was always crowded in summer with the members of a large family. They folded laundry, darned socks, salted green apples from their trees, and taught us younger ones how to make lanterns from the splintered wood cartons the raspberries came in. There were a lot of sisters and they were always happy and laughing even with no fellows hanging around. You see, they were different. Their father was an apostle and their mother was always home and the spirit you felt there was like walking into church during a good meeting.

My favorite was Angelyn, who led the singing in

Sunday School with a perpetual smile and a lot of vigorous arm action. One Sunday at the end of the undisciplined days of summer, Angelyn had us practice over and again and yet again the hymn that contained the startling counsel, "Before you make a promise, consider well its importance; and when made (long pause) engrave it upon your heart (faster)."

In those days, hymns and their messages fluttered from my mind in the wake of a friend's giggle. But not when Angelyn roused us with that reminder.

I was soon to put this philosophy to the test. Mother had bought me a new winter coat on the off-season sale that gave you a discount if you tossed in an old coat for the poor, the sick, or the afflicted. I thought it an elegant coat—a whole bodice of fake fur with lovely green napped wool below. And it wasn't a hand-me-down! I wanted to go at once and model it for Enid. The firm instructions were that I was to wait until after dinner. I begged. Mother held her ground with the annoying question, "Promise?" Silently I figured by the time Mother hassled with my little brother at the bathroom basin, I could be down to Enid's and back. I knew I had promised her, but—

On the way back, haste made jelly of my legs and I fell full length in the mud puddled with the overflow of Mr. Noall's hose. My new coat was a mess. Such swift reprisal! In my mind I could hear Angelyn's voice lilting that serious business about promises, and I was suddenly certain Somebody Up There must be keeping track.

When I got home Mother took one look at my soiled new coat and cried, "Oh! Elaine!" with such dismay I wanted to blend into the blue blossoms sprinkling the sunporch walls where all the family sat at meal.

With a loud rip Mother tore off a piece of old Turkish toweling and attacked that soiled coat on me with such vengeance and unwomanly strength I was sure my skin would peel off too. Beads of perspiration dampened her

forehead so close now to mine. Periodically she'd repeat,
"Oh! Elaine!"

Well, I never knew my name could mean so many
things: fury, despair, disappointment, fatigue. When I
couldn't stop crying, her tears blended with mine at last,
and my name meant forgiveness when Mother finally
sighed it softly, wrapping me to her.

But I never liked the coat after that. It was a reminder
of the promise I'd broken.

One of the best things about going to church in the
summer was that everybody stood around in the cool
evening and talked after. The boys would try to walk the
narrow ledge separating the foundation from the
stonework. The girls would giggle and finger each other's
organdy sashes, trying to untie the bows without getting
caught. And because parents were relaxed, we kids knew
we'd get them to let us sleep out in somebody's backyard.

"Behave yourself," Mother would counsel as we'd
strut off into a summer's night, straggling our blankets
behind us. "Now behave," she always called again.

But one time I guess I didn't. Instead of sleeping out,
we had our slumber party in the freshly finished basement
recreation room of a family whose standard of living far
surpassed most of ours. A recreation room was a brand-new
luxury. After all, what was recreation? All we ever heard
about was work in those days. There was even a comic strip
called "Tillie the Toiler." Recreation as a way of life was so
far from our thinking that we equated it with the resurrection and let it go at that. But whatever they called that
room, it was all clean and cool, calcimined and con-
goleumized, and we were excited about trying it out.

The next morning we were sitting around playing
"Touring" and I guess I did something that turned the
lady of the house into something I was glad my own
mother wasn't. She suddenly yanked me by my arm and
stretched me up the steps to the back door and then bodily

34

shoved me out. I turned back to her in shock to get an explanation, to protest my innocence, or to apologize, at least, as I'd always been taught to do, for whatever I'd done wrong. That was my mistake. When I looked into her face it was the ugliest I'd ever seen, contorted, as she spat out the words, "I hate you! I hate you! I hate you!" And she slammed the door.

Summer hung heavy in the heat of her hate.

I don't think I'd ever heard anybody say that before—to me at least—and mean it. I didn't know people could feel that way about other people. I thought all mothers were perfect and loved all little children.

It was so awful I wanted to die. But I didn't. I stood there in a kind of trance for a time and then turned and walked down the long driveway, seeing everything with a strange new clarity. The grass between the cement strips wasn't worn in spots like ours. The black-eyed susans were shredded on the edge the car brushed by. A parade of ants marched with a long skinny straw stick. I walked on past the hollyhocks we made dolls from with toothpicks, past the mint bed, and down the slope to the street, fingering the lint in my pocket into a tight ball, licking my lips and rubbing them dry with the back of my hand, only to lick them again.

The Woolley twins played on their huge front steps with the metal banisters bent like the G clef. The Ashton baby was having a sunbath and a blonde girl who kept to herself was sitting in their wooden swing writing her never-ending poetry. And none of them cared that I wanted to die, that hate had squashed my heart and put butterflies where my stomach was supposed to be.

I walked past them all and I didn't cry until I saw Mother. And oh, how I wished I were still small enough to sit on her lap and be cradled in her arms. Yet she comforted me, letting me cry a bit, waiting before she asked, "Whatever is the matter with my girl?"

How do you describe hate when it isn't in your vocabulary? How do you communicate heartbreak when you are so new at it?

Mother waited. The clock ticked. A fly buzzed around, and I was conscious now of Mother's person and knew she loved me even though I never could tell her I was hated already. The sobbing subsided and finally she leaned back, looked into my eyes, and wisely dismissed the whole trauma with, "Well, Elaine, I've learned that when you are handed a lemon, make lemonade out of it."

And she went back to canning cherries, leaving me with my thoughts.

I stayed away from that house with the recreation room all week. Next Sunday when that lady flounced into church all super charming, pursing her lips and sucking in her cheeks at the people she met, I wasn't impressed. I'd seen her ugly, as ugly as if she had eaten a hundred lemons. It would take a powerful portion of sugar, all right, to make a good lemonade mix out of her.

But that was it. When people deserve it least is when they need sweetness most, and I knew I didn't want to make anybody feel as she'd made me feel, ever, no matter how they misbehaved. So I smiled my sweetest to her and went in to join the congregation. And do you know what Angelyn had them singing that day? "Angry words, oh, let them never. . ."

Chapter Seven

Curious Learnings

*F*or years summer began the first Monday after school was out when a fluffy white-haired neighbor lady gathered us girls to help her with the Costumes. We followed her from house to house, Pied-Piper style, panting to keep pace with her. Bits of satin, an old Army coat, feathers, and gauzy flowers were collected along with us girls. By getting to us before we were involved in anything else, she was assured a bit of our help. But we didn't understand that psychology then. We only knew we were needed for the world's most exciting project—readying costumes in case somebody needed them for the Primary Pageant or the Covered Wagon Day parade.

We threaded elastic and pressed seams. She created costumes, all the while singsonging plans for elaborate productions that may or may not materialize. We were spellbound but we tired long before she did. When we finally gave out, our Costume General would pass the cookies and then march us all home. Only it wasn't a march. It was more like a dance because she kept doing a little twirl to encourage the laggers.

There came a summer when I felt too mature for this sort of thing. Mother understood but urged that I go just one more time in an act of appreciation.

"Make her feel your thanks and observe her carefully this time," Mother counseled. "Someday you'll remember that growing old isn't so bad if you stay young."

But staying young didn't seem relevant to me then. I was young. I was immortal. Nothing would ever change.

It did, however, with the appearance in our lives of Blye, who quickly taught me some advantages of growing older. Blye was one of the small-town girls who came to the city to attend summer sessions at the business college at the bottom of the Hill. These girls would find live-in situations with families close by and they'd help around the house in exchange for board and room. Our Blye turned out to be just another member of the family. She shared my room and I learned some curious things about being glamorous from her. She read movie magazines and tried all of the Secrets of the Stars. I watched her roll her hair on kid curlers with a setting gel she made by cooking flaxseed. I saw her rub Vaseline darkened with a melted brown crayon on her lashes and she plucked out all of her eyebrows—unheard-of things to do in our neighborhood. She rubbed lemons—precious lemons!—onto her heels and elbows and knuckles. She used K-lotion and glycerine on her hands and Hind's Honey and Almond Cream on her face. She buffed her nails until I thought they would go up in smoke. But the most exciting thing of all was her pink taffeta dress that was shorter in front than in back. The blue satin lining in back framed her legs elegantly and swept to the floor when she walked. She wore it to the stag dances every Saturday night at Coconut Grove, Salt Lake's answer to Hollywood's seat of excitement. To a girl from the settlement of Santaquin down south, this was something wonderful. To Mother it was a hazard, and she kept a close check.

In the way children have of uncovering things, we discovered that poor Blye couldn't see except up close, and we would ask her the time just so we could watch her squint down with her nose practically on the face of the clock. Then we'd burst into laughter. It happened that Mother got in on one of those disgraceful sessions and shamed us thoroughly. But she learned that Blye needed glasses badly and didn't have the money to get them.

We held a family council later, when Blye was away, and talked about the help she had been to us. Daddy liked the way she giggled at his old jokes and kept his glass filled with water at dinner. Junior said she'd shined his shoes for Sunday School. I was enchanted with the fingerwave (using flaxseed gel!) she'd given me for Beverly's birthday party. Lowell said she wasn't too bad for a girl, and little Nadine clapped for everything. With appreciation and sympathy for her plight and noble unselfishness welling up in our hearts, we decided to finance her trip to the eye doctor. We did it by canceling the family outing to Saltair on the edge of the Great Salt Lake with its enormously exciting giant racer.

I'll never forget the night Dad presented Blye with the finished glasses. She slowly put them on. "What time is it?" we all cried. And Blye looked at that clock from where she sat across the room and told us the time. Then she burst into tears.

Charity beyond the family—sisterhood when you had different parents—she hadn't complained when we teased nor because she couldn't see—how rude we'd been to laugh at her plight—how good it felt to make someone happy. . .these thoughts whirled through my mind as we all sat there silent through her tears. Then I hugged Blye, I was so happy for her, and then everbody hugged everybody else and Mother brought in one of Jello's new "six delicious flavors" with whipped cream and sliced bananas for a treat.

41

A few years later Mother made me my first formal and I chose pink taffeta in honor of Blye. There were two dozen tiny lavender crystal buttons down the back placket but no zipper. Zippers were new and Mother hadn't learned how to insert one, so she sewed me into each dress she made for me each time I wore it—including this pink taffeta. When the doorbell rang she had just finished "sewing me in" and I flew to the door, unrestrained. The porch was empty. Suddenly a tomato hit against the screen door and splattered little black and red specks all over the front of my dress. Then I heard some of the neighborhood boys guffawing as they ran by, taunting me about going out with a boy who lived off the Hill. In their tracks appeared my date and my heart sank. It was my only formal. There wasn't time to get unsewn, cleaned, resewn. I was standing where he could see me, anyway.

"The options are clear," Mother said matter-of-factly. "You can stay home in false pride and ruin a nice evening or forget yourself and smile a lot. No one will notice the spots then."

So I smiled. I even smiled when I saw those jokesters at church the next day.

But that summer I mastered the sewing skill of inserting a zipper.

Chapter Eight

A Little Out Of The Sun

Summer rain was precious in our desert valley. Even a mid-August mist was cause for a celebration. It was the great common denominator, too. People would stand on their porches in a down-pour smiling broadly and waving across the torrents tirelessly. Rain was vital for the crops, for our cool—and for us kids it determined whether the clay cave could be played in.

The first thing we did in a rainstorm was "eagle claws" with a ball bat. The one whose hand grasp reached the lip on the bat handle last was declared official judge of the clay's readiness. We used that system for solving all kinds of important arguments, like who had to wash the dishes instead of wipe, who got to post the flag on the porch pillar for the Fourth, and who sat next to Grandma at Sunday dinner. (This latter was a dubious privilege, because she'd make us clean our plates till they looked "slicked licked," and yet we could quietly examine the holes in her ears where her jewelry hung until our curiosity was thoroughly satiated.)

Well, when the "heavens opened good and proper,"

as Mr. Korth used to say, pontificating after the fact, we'd wait a couple of hours and then start haunting the small cave on the side of the hill off Wall Street. We'd scoop up a handful of earth and mash it between our fingers, debating its readiness. Ground rules were that we could give an opinion but we had to wait for an official decision from our "judge." Timing was so critical. When the rain seepage had reached the clay bed, you just had to be on hand. Too long a wait meant the clay would crumble. Too soon and the stuff wasn't moist enough. After a summer storm you just had to stall chores and forgo outings if you cared about clay. I cared about clay.

I got so I could pretty well tell when it was going to rain. First I'd watch for a yellow sunset. A yellow sunset was more than a fisherman's warning, it was an absolutely summer novelty over our Great Salt Lake where the sun went down like thunder in the summer and the skies were fired past bedtime. A yellow sunset was sign of a storm, and the sulphur smells would rise from the lake. Next I'd check Woolley's poplar trees for verification. When the white side of the leaves showed we'd get out the umbrellas for the morrow.

I remember one time when the storm was so spectacular the dried June grass couldn't hold the soil and rivulets wrinkled the hill. The neighbors talked of a mud flood and the Capitol flower beds had to be built up all over again. But the quality of the clay in the cave was never better. Why, it was like I had magic in my hands, and the fever of creation raced my pulse. I was oblivious to present company as I squeezed, pinched, and patted my own reasonable facsimile of Massasoit, who at that time graced the Capitol rotunda. This heroic-size bronze statue was our introduction to sculpture and heightened our reverence for the integrity of the American Indian. Massasoit was the Indian chief who first greeted the Pilgrims. The fact that Cyrus Dallin, a native Utahn, had created this monument for faraway Plymouth Rock was impressive to me. So, sheltered though we were, the near nudity of this massive statue never embarrassed us, much less fascinated us unduly.

But it greatly disturbed one of the old maids who lived nearby to see me sculpting a naked man when she crossed the street to give the message that I was wanted for dinner. She was an important church worker and made sure we said our prayers when we slept over with her niece. And of course since she didn't play around the Capitol, how could she know a Massasoit when she saw one? She made such a fuss about the "goings on" in that cave with "innocent children" that it was declared out-of-bounds by all the parents.

Mother's pride was fierce, and she couldn't bear the thought that her "lovely little daughter" had been misjudged, she was sure! You see, when I explained to Mother about Massasoit, she walked me right back to the cave to hunt for the sculpture that had been dropped during the trauma of a "lady apostle's" (as we called her behind her back) lecture on virtue. Mother wanted to see my work for herself.

47

We found Massasoit all right, miraculously all of a piece though somewhat misshapen. Mother handled it very carefully, smoothing the cold, damp surface of the unfinished, innocent work, She turned it around and around thoughtfully. Her smile was kind. Her eyes even lit up some but then saddened.

"Look, Elaine, this is very nicely done. Why don't you hurry up and make a feather for his headband and get a loincloth in place. Then we'll walk over to Sister Beesley's home to show her what you really had in mind. You might even want to scratch your signature in the clay and make her a present of it."

She didn't want the sculpture, but Mother was satisfied that the dear sister understood my intentions.

Needless to say, I did not grow up to become a native Utah sculptor with my work in far places. Anyway, for me it was more important that I come to an understanding of viewpoint. Perspective. Michelangelo portrayed Christ dead in his *Pieta*. Thorvaldson saw him living in his *Christus*. And being positive was better than being negative, Mother explained, as we studied pictures of the beautiful works of the master sculptors.

But I didn't go back to the cave again, and seldom did a summer have so many good rains.

There was another side to summer storms and that was what they did to sandbox castles and playhouses.

For a proper playhouse, we'd take all day to drape blankets, old curtains, and burlap bags the canning sugar came in. We'd swag them from fruit tree to fruit tree, to the clothesline pole and back again, with room after room being bounded by the beginnings and endings of blankets and burlap. By the time we'd finish the hang-and-tie treatment, it was day's end and I'd usually check the sunset so I could try to pray away the yellow if it showed in the west.

One day we had put up a particularly elaborate affair with plans to hold our club meetings there until the weekend, when it would have to come down so the lawn could be cut. We even designated a portion of it as a tent to hide the boys' rubber guns. This way they wouldn't pester our plans and Daddy couldn't confiscate the guns, which had been declared dangerous weapons. The rubber gun was notched out of a wooden crate with a newfangled spring clothes pin nailed at the trigger end. The boys cut narrow strips of old inner tube, which were stretched from the gun point and secured in the clothes pin. When you pinched the pin, it released the rubber. That ammunition could sting if you were a target and it hit its mark! Naturally this ingenious item did not win a parental seal of approval, so the playhouse was a great new cache.

The dawn after these labors, I think I smelled the rain before I heard it, and I tightened my eyes firmly against waking to the reality of ruin in our backyard. I lay there for long minutes considering what to do. I could bury my face in my pillow and sleep out the storm, or I could get up and watch the destruction take place. I got up.

I remember standing there mentally reciting in rhythm with the rain "On a misty, moisty morning when cloudy was the weather. . ." I said that nursery rhyme over and over pointlessly. I kept wishing some old man in leather would come along to save the sog from happening to our blankets sopping it up out there.

Instead my older brother appeared sleepily by my side. "It's a mess, isn't it."

Why did he have to say it out loud like that? Once labeled, that's also what I saw it as. It was indeed a miserable mess that we would have to clean up. Of course I began to cry.

"Oh, what are you kicking about?" he asked flatly. "Half the fun was getting it up."

Well, you don't forget insight like that!

That same brother talked me through many a storm in life, and as the years passed he emerged as my hero, my knight, my prince charming, my dreamboat. Very early I resigned myself to the second-citizen class for husband material because I figured there simply wasn't anybody else that smart around.

Or good-looking.

When he graduated from high school, I followed him every place he'd let me while he got ready. High school seniors in those days didn't have caps and gowns for commencement. They cost money to rent. And who had money like that? Graduation was usually the time a boy acquired his first suit. Or he borrowed one.

Junior's was a brown blazer with white flannel slacks that he wore with argyle socks and saddle shoes. We'd all sacrificed some for that outfit but it was worth it. He was splendid. I gazed fondly, chin in hand, while he tied and retied his tie, combed and recombed his hair so it would slick straight back from his brow. Then he posed for a Kodak shot trying hard not to smile.

"Stand a little out of my sun," he said grandly, giving me a gentle jab in the ribs. Then he rewarded my worship by adding, "and thanks, in advance, beautiful, for not telling anyone I put Vaseline on my hair."

Beautiful! Me? To him? Oh, what an absolutely marvelous night. Why, I'd stand a little out of the sun, walk through the rain, anything at all—except clean out the garbage closet—for that brother!

Chapter Nine

To Every Thing
A Season

The summer Stanley killed himself was the first time personal death seemed a real possibility to me. He was just our age and had hung himself from the hot water pipe crossing the ceiling of their basement apartment. If it could happen to Stanley. . .

Everyone who had ignored him in life was curiously interested in him at death. People crowded the funeral but the few vases of zinnias and cosmos plus the funeral wreath from the bishop did little to dispel the gloom.

We didn't know where his father was. Mother says maybe that was one reason his mom carried on so. Daddy said she didn't know any better since they never came to church. Anyway, her sobs and wails railed against my ear and assaulted my heart. She hung over his coffin, clinging to his poor stiff body, flattening the paper lilies as she struggled to hold him to her. She kept calling him "My baby," and the bishop kept tugging at her shoulders, mumbling, "Come, sister."

I lingered, frankly staring. I wondered how I could help. For I yearned to help, to heal her, to remind her that her son would be just fine with Heavenly Father. She was much older than I but it seemed she hadn't learned that yet. Besides, I couldn't figure out why she fought so frantically for a boy who had chosen to leave her. All the sobs in the kingdom wouldn't open his eyes or bring her another chance to rectify her neglect of him. Anyway, if he weren't already dead, he'd have suffocated under her heavy black veils drowned in Evening in Paris. She was the first woman I'd ever seen up close who wore rouge like that.

"To every thing there is a season," the Bishop said at last, "a time to get and a time to lose." That mother's moans punctuating Ecclesiastes wounded me—not because she had lost Stanley, but because Stanley had been driven to death. It was all wrong. Life was to be lived with whatever options. Grieving at the grave was ill-timed. I believe it was then that I experienced deep inside me my first sweet response to blessing counting.

Brother Richmond taught a lesson on the resurrection the next Sunday, and while he never had more rapt attention, it wasn't until Betty's sister LaPreal died of sleeping sickness a couple of years later that we learned of dignity in death. The peace of that service was its own defense for good living.

One summer the man across the street brought home a new mother for his children. She had never been married before, and we wondered at her stenographer's clothes and her sleek Carole Lombard hairdo. She didn't seem up to the brood of boys who ran around half dressed and barefoot on rainy days and sultry spells alike. Mother often commented that in spite of their casual ways, those children didn't have the sickness we did.

We could see their property from our sun porch, as we called it, and we'd press our noses against the glass to watch their adventures in a tree house with its own rope swing and a dugout in the field for potato bakes. The father seemed to be gone a lot after the first while. How she

54

managed inside we could only imagine, but outside the boys paid no heed to her gentle pleas.

In time she changed—hair, figure, clothes, demeanor. Some toddlers of her own swelled the ranks of the family and the size of her hips. Then one day she died. It was interesting to watch the way those boys shaped up in such a hurry. They carried her coffin, ordered flowers to be sent, and took the younger children in hand. What it amounted to was that she was missed. By the time the McMasters had finished singing "I walk in the garden alone" at the funeral, those boys were all bawling.

Some people dismissed her death as a blessing and a deserved rest, but the family found that they had lost their best friend. What they hadn't done for her in life, they hustled to do for her in death. Their place took on a shine at last, but it seemed to me it was too little too late, and so for nearly a week I helped Mother with the dishes without being told.

Chapter Ten

The Wages Of Work

*O*ne summer I learned a secret about work. It was a summer in the dark depression years, and my friend Enid had lost ten precious dollars that had been entrusted to her to pay on an overdue account. She was trying to earn it back ironing napkins and hankies for Mrs. Knight.

The fierce loyalty of friendship that summer breeds demanded I go through this ordeal with her. The job was hers, however, so she ironed. I sat there and figured out the swiftest, safest, and most successful way to smooth, stretch, and fold a delicate linen square. Whatever I said, she tried to do. We wasted a lot of precious hours away from our retreat behind the bridal wreath until we finally learned that if a job is worth doing, it is worth doing well. You don't have to re-iron so many napkins so many times that way.

That was the summer of the tramps. The whole country seemed on the move because jobs were scarce and people were testing the "grass is greener" myth. Men down on their luck slept in nearby Pioneer Park and hung around the railroad tracks waiting for the next boxcar to move them along.

Our house was on the edge of the hill above the tracks, and often men would knock at our door for a handout. Mother never refused them a meal, and she usually got them talking about their mothers and encouraged them to go home. Once in a while a young man would cry, and I felt that running away from home was most dreadful.

I remember one fellow's asking if he could wash with the garden hose first before he ate. I watched him pull off his dusty shirt, gulp in the clean water, splash it about his neck and face, and scrub it under his arms. Mother was so impressed that she served his food on a dinner plate instead of the customary pie pan. And she told him if he'd work industriously along the back fence and free the forsythia from the choking wild morning glory, she'd give him fifty cents. And she did!

It was then I sensed that cleanliness has its own rewards and that it isn't so much what happens to you as what you do about it.

The summer I finished grade school, I began tending children. The first wage I received was the golden pouch to independence. I raced down the hill to the drugstore by Temple Square. I had passed that store twice a day to and from school for seven years, drooling over the candy counter in agony. Money from Mother was always accompanied by the firm instruction, "Don't spend it on candy. Promise?" And I'd keep my promise and eat peanuts while everyone else ate candy to their heart's content.

So that day I squandered my earnings—less ten per cent for tithes held out like a good Mormon girl. I bought seven Snickers and a Powerhouse at five cents each, and I ate all those bars going back up the hill. If only I'd savored them some. Maybe if it hadn't been so hot, things would have been different. Anyway, I was so churned up inside by the time I reached the edge of the Capitol grounds, I thought I'd never see home again. It wasn't the sickness that taught me a lesson, though; it was the total lack of satisfaction in lonely self-indulgence.

My first steady tending job was at the Petersons'. They were renters and that set them apart on the Hill. What made them different to me, though, was the way their house was. There were always dishes and stale food piled all over the table, sink, and countertops. The draperies were never open when I arrived. The only decorative thing in the house was a tied and dyed velvet shawl thrown over a square table. At its center was a fruit jar that had been covered with pictures glued with sand sparkles. and it held some cattail stalks dipped in blue food coloring. There wasn't a book in the place either, even though Mr. Peterson was a traveling salesman for *My Bookhouse* books for children, so I would carry a sack of things to entertain the little girl. Mrs. Peterson didn't smile much, and I was glad when I could go home and had, as Mother reminded me each time, done "my duty."

It was weeks before I overheard a neighbor say that Mr. Peterson never came home because he made friends with his lady customers along the way. But one day he came home before Mrs. Peterson did. He didn't have to tell me who he was. I could tell by the way his little girl ran to him. There were smiles wreathing the windows that afternoon. Until the mother returned. Then the quarreling began as if I were only part of the pitiful furniture. It wasn't like that at our home when my Daddy came back from a train trip. We all scrambled to get the first hug, to feel the secret places of his pockets where the inevitable small surprises were hidden. And Mother stood by laughing and laughing until Daddy silenced her with kisses.

I felt sorry for Mrs. Peterson when the divorce came, but it seemed to me that home ought to be a place a man wanted to hurry back to, and that the real wages for work should be joy.

Chapter Eleven

And What Of Structured Summers?

*S*tructured summers were the strength behind character development, according to Mrs. Baggley. By April her children knew exactly what they'd be doing each hour of the day through the vacation period. The schedule was mounted on the cupboard door where the drinking glasses were kept. An indelible pencil on a string was touched to the tongue to write purple as the children checked off their practicing, their chores, their various kinds of lessons. Including elocution. By the time 4:30 dragged around and the schedule read "relax with friends," the friends weren't around. As summer progressed, my friend's pencil licks became juicier and each "x" bolder. She hated summer.

For me the weeks flew by.

Mother used to give us a hug and remark, "The teachers have you all winter. Come summer, you're mine."

And what a time we had together. We'd take the open train to the Great Salt Lake to "refresh safety factors for our environment." That meant being reminded to keep our heads high until we felt ourselves floating like a cork on the buoyant water. It also meant not gulping any salt water and remembering to lick a finger to remove the salt splashed into our eyes before it would burn too much. We'd come home crusted white around our ears, our swim suits stiff, and our toes stuck with brine shrimp, but we loved it.

In late afternoon we always got cleaned up, and often we'd walk past Temple Square to the public library. Each time Mother would point out the "hand" carved by one of our ancestors on the temple. We felt a personal interest in that building very early. Sometimes we cooked pancakes over an open fire in City Creek Canyon because everyone should know how to build a proper campfire, and how to put it out, too. There were sessions with Mother's book on painting before we toured the current art show hanging in the Capitol gallery. My favorite was early morning visits to farmers' market for fresh produce. Sometimes Daddy would go along because he felt it was imperative to know a good watermelon when you thumped one. That's what summer is all about!

But there came a summer when Mother felt I needed some formal training. She promised I would be popular when I grew up if I knew how to play the piano. Maybe, but getting there was its own kind of torture for me. The lessons would begin after Easter to "get a good start on the season." Each summer Mother had fresh hope for the miracle that would turn me into an accomplished pianist. She would have loved such an opportunity herself. I just wanted to be popular.

Mrs. Hanks was my first teacher, and I loved her. I had to walk two blocks and past a mean dog to her house, so I was sticky and beady when I got there. She was gentle and patient with my meager efforts at practice. Along about mid-July she complained, "Elaine, if only you could sit still maybe I could teach you something." My only reaction to this was wonderment that she herself could sit so still so long inside by that brown upright when outside there was so much to revel in.

Then I had a man teacher. He operated on the music-in-your-own-home basis, but home was the last place I wanted to be if he were going to be there. But since he didn't get his dollar unless he gave the lesson, he soon started tracking me down at my haunts.

My stomach flip-flopped when I had to climb in his Hudson in front of my friends after school. You see, nobody rode home unless he was sick and his mother had to come for him. Walking home in sweeping crowds was a big part of our social life at that age. I mean, *Everybody* walked. Even Frankie, with crutches his constant companions, hiked up that hill from school every day.

Come summer my teacher would cruise around the confines of my world to find me. If we were at Mr. Mace's store, I'd stall by making lengthy comparisons between the garish pink and green syrup-filled wax teeth. If I had been swimming at the Deseret Gym and saw that Hudson coming up the hill, I'd brave stinging nettle or the gummy stick of field burrs by cutting through vacant lots to avoid ultimate confrontation as long as possible.

Though stick-to-itiveness was a quality Mother felt I needed, this teacher and I suffered equally during this period.

Later I had a real professional musician at the McCune School of Music and Art there on the side of the Hill. She filled my heart with a love of music. Her method was Motivation—she played a lot for me. She played "Romance" by Sibelius, gently pointing out the girl's voice, then the boy's voice as suggested by the music. I was carried away by that imagery and I delighted at how I felt inside as she played. But I couldn't abide how the piece sounded when I tackled it. I guess it finally got to my teacher too, because one day she stood behind me while I struggled and spoke the lines that called a halt forever to further formal piano lessons for me.

"Elaine," she said carefully, "you have such nice broad shoulders, such beautiful long fingers and big, strong hands. You could be a fine pianist if only—"

I thought she was going to say, "if only you would practice." Instead she lamented, "—if only you had talent!"

I didn't master the piano, but I learned that summer that people are good at different things and there is no point in running if you are on the wrong road. And structuring a summer could never change that.

Chapter Twelve

Come Summer,
Stay Summer

*S*ummers were great because you mixed with People. You weren't locked into steamy schoolrooms with everyone your own age. Mixing with People let you know what you liked and what you didn't about the way grown-ups grew up.

I liked Rosabel.

She was the first emancipated woman I'd ever met. In the first place, I never saw her in a housedress. She wore jewelry in the morning with sweaters that matched her skirts. And she owned her very own typewriter. And she was writing a novel.

She also organized the Women's League for Self-Preservation (or something like that), which had the whole hill buzzing the best part of one summer. I don't know how she managed it in a conservative neighborhood like ours, but she even had some of the grandmothers involved. Before we could shout, "Peace at any price!" with proper isolationist intonation, we were sawing off old brooms to shoulder-like guns during drill and saving for oxfords. Our uniform was a white blouse and dark skirt with a black bandeleau. And oxfords.

While Hitler was marching across Europe, we were prancing up and down the dimly lit caverns of the old City and County Building after hours. This fragile lady with her back in a brace from some ancient injury would call the commands to this strange crowd of sister patriots. Her voice was whispery hoarse and her orders came forth like a slip of the tongue. She was such an uncertain trumpet, we didn't dare giggle or talk or we would miss the command and collisions would occur.

The marching ended with the summer, but the memories of her instructions on posture and "being anxiously engaged in a good cause" persisted because she was such a study in contrasts. She also was a widow raising a big family, and as Mother carefully reminded me, what counted was that her children were "turning out right."

Another thing about summers in those days is that people lived outdoors and you could watch them with each other. You could see how their wash looked and what they did when the children were naughty. You learned family schedules by the time someone came out to water the lawn or shake the rugs. And their problems were hard to hide. So was the way they dealt with them.

Down the street from us lived a family with a father so jovial and interested in each of us that you'd never guess he'd been the hardest hit in the depression. That is, unless you saw his furniture being carried out at periodic intervals to placate bill collectors. The word spread like a June-grass fire that the haulers were at that door again. All the kids showed up to watch what would be carried out this time. We saw the piano go. And the round oak table and matching chairs and buffet from the dining room. The only things finally left in the front rooms were a rocker and the precious Majestic radio we stretched in front of to listen to "Myrt 'n' Marge" and "Jack Benny." The Victorola was used as a phone stand in the kitchen. A family has to live.

Each time the movers finished their unhappy task, this man would chuck his wife under the chin and say with a half smile, "So. . ." Then quick as could be he'd pile all of us kids into his DeSoto and we'd sing "I've been working on the railroad" all the way to the A & W stand for root beer all around. Maybe he couldn't build us a playground, but he surely taught us plenty about coping.

It was early summer when the fire at the Jex house broke out. The sirens gave the signal, the spirals of smoke marked the place, and the neighborhood moved in to keep vigil. A house being eaten by licks of fire is a nightmare itself. But to lose one's house and belongings in those troubled times had all the grown-ups weeping empathetically. And there was more. The Jex boy was leaving for a mission in a few days.

It takes cash for a mission and Frank had helped to earn his share by half-soling shoes for those of us needing it. For the richer people he had made custom silver bracelets with their names punched out on the hand.

When the burning roof started to cave in, something must have snapped inside Frank's sobbing sister's heart, for suddenly she darted through the Boy Scout crowd-control barrier and up the stairs into that inferno.

A gasp went up from the crowd and then people began giving each other orders. Before anyone could be convinced to be a hero, out Lois came again, singed but victorious. She had Frank's one suit! It was a miracle. He could still go on his mission. She also brought out only one of his new shoes, which brought the release of laughter.

I was impressed at her courage but full of wonder that she seemed so uncomfortable in the attention and limelight that followed. "Anybody would have done it," she repeated into her hands covering her face. But I knew I wouldn't have.

"Come summer," I used to say. "Come summer, I'll be good at Allsies in jacks." Or, "Come summer I'll finish my knitting. Come summer I'll be beautiful. Come summer I'll be half through my novel like Rosabel. Come summer I'll be selfless as Lois." Come Summer. Stay!

But the summers came and went, with my life not equal to my resolutions. Still the days dawned bright for me always, and joy in just being alive matched the marvelous season.

Chapter Thirteen

The Green Summer

*W*e sensed summer almost before it came to the Hill. We waited for it so long. Then one day the wind blew warm out of City Creek Canyon and rippled the June grass, new green and fragrant, with the sweet juice of the feathery spikes ready for our sucking.

One day our weeping willow would be the loveliest yellow-green as the sap ran high to the twig tips, but the next day, it seemed, there was its blessed shade like a merciful healer. The willow was supple and willing in the whims of the wind. It became my symbol of summer because it was the first green of spring and the last green of fall. Summer lingered longer with a willow around.

"Watch the willow if you want to stretch the summers of your life," Daddy would philosophize each season's end when the graceful tree finally dropped a leaf and whispered of winter, " 'for summer's lease hath all too short a date.' "

But I thought the green summers of my life would last forever that first time I hiked Ensign Peak alone. I set out way before sunrise on a most spectacularly beautiful

June morning. We had climbed that beehive-shaped mountain as a family, as a church group, as a gang with sack lunches squashed down into the sweaters tied about our waists. This day my aloneness was exhilarating as I made my way to the top. This was no small hill and the perspective of my neighborhood below reminded me of the soap city I had carved of Salt Lake when I was twelve. I sat looking down at the houses I knew so well and at their people beginning to stir with the sun. Cars backed out, sprinklers splashed on, the trolley clanged up from town. I watched the achingly familiar scenes as an extension of myself. Yet, it was like being God, seeing the whole picture. Seeing but not being seen.

There was Doc's house—Doc, who, getting us trapped and speechless, filled our cavities and our minds at the same time. With rare good humor he counseled us strongly about personal standards. How could you let someone like Doc down?

Mercedes' place was strangely quiet. Usually it brimmed with people of all ages on all kinds of occasions and all feeling the warmth of special graciousness. The worth of souls was something this family believed in and I liked to be there so much I'd promised myself to name one of my children after one of theirs someday. And I did!

Lincoln's home was hidden with trees but I knew it was there with its broad porch facing the valley south. Like Lincoln, it was open and welcoming. Who on the Hill had not felt his arm as we faltered in public performance, wavered in want, or struggled to resolve the problems of life?

Anna's place—humble, gifted Anna who ate away her lonely singleness. Didn't any of us think of Anna? Yet her little poems, written to meet a need, were sent by the hundreds. She taught me that I had an obligation to put on paper the feelings that crowded my heart, and she shared her secret of how to write in the dark if a special idea awakened you from sleep.

Finally I let myself look upon our own white stucco house, the scene of my most tender times, my greatest learnings. Almost in panic I realized how small it looked and with a wrench of my heart I felt it slipping from my life.

Everywhere I looked there was someone who had touched my life. At sixteen I was the sum of all of them. My heart flooded with gratitude and a new awareness. I had some debts to pay.

In 1847 Brigham Young had raised an ensign to the Lord here on this peak, according to the plaque on top. Well, I raised my own that day and came down from the mount determined to be useful.

Summer stretches for the child from fresh freedom past endless adventures in a unique alliance with nature. For the grown-up, summer is the symbol of fruition. At seventeen I felt very grown up. I was about to have my patriarchal blessing. There had been fasting and prayer and deep discussions about the meaning of it all with my parents and my boyfriend. It was summer's time of roses, mock orange and honeysuckle sweetening the air. Everything was at its best and I wanted to be.

The night before my appointment with Patriarch Jones I felt a strong need to gather myself together with Heavenly Father. I went quickly out the screened door and stood there for a time listening to the summers of my youth sift by on the night song of the crickets. Then I felt once again the pull of the stars. Shyly at first I lay down on my back on prickly grass as I had done so often as a child. Once again I took a deep breath and turned my face skyward, breathing Millay's phrase I'd memorized in English— "O world, I cannot hold thee close enough." Once again I studied the heavens, finding the familiar constellations, getting placement with the North Star. Then finally, the mind-stretching, soul-searing experience of being lifted into the universe—almost into the presence of God—set my heart to pounding.

My prayers that night got through. The witness of the Spirit that God lives and cares and was mindful of little me warmed me to tears. That was a green summer—the beginning of my trying to make decisions according to God's will for me and committing myself to a way of life that would ensure fulfillment of his sacred promises. What better gift from a summer?

Chapter Fourteen

Beyond The Hill

There was the summer of love just before "our" war. The serious rumblings that echoed across oceans were crowded from my heart by one older boy. I operated at fever level with a sweeping love for life, friends, and my family, for tennis, for twilight and the morning skies, for poetry, and for Glenn Miller himself, whose music accompanied almost every move I made. I painted my nails to "String of Pearls" and beat fudge to the rhythm of "Little Brown Jug." But "Sunrise Serenade" was "our" song and I'd play it over and over again while I'd record the details of my life in a five-year diary with a lock and key.

His name filled the pages. There was summer in his voice and every word he uttered in my presence, the way his hair swirled from the crown of his head, his strong jawline and one injured thumbnail, all found place in my diary. Clippings of his basketball games were stuffed in the back. If he laughed at something somebody said, I laughed too. Only I wished I'd said such a clever thing so he'd find pleasure in me. If he shifted to tenor in the campfire sing-along, I'd shift to alto for closer harmony. I said his name like a prayer when I fell off to sleep and I practiced writing it with "Mrs." in front of it, sometimes with a fancy flourish, sometimes with a cool, sophisticated slant.

All of this emotional involvement on my part while he went on tossing the *Deseret News* on the porches of the Hill without a pause before our door.

One night at a church dance a miracle occurred. He asked me to dance. My moment had arrived and all the articles I'd read on charm were now to be applied. I would impress him. He would never forget me. What actually happened was that I began chattering to reveal to him my clever wit and brilliance, my darling personality.

Very shortly he stopped dancing, moved away from me though still holding me in his arms, and said, with the patience and wisdom of Age, "Elaine, one doesn't talk during 'Stardust'."

One doesn't talk during "Stardust"! All the passion of my heart rushed to my throat and lodged there. I resolved then and there to dedicate my life to helping girls understand what really worked with boys. Obviously my own authorities had been wrong.

There came a time shortly after when I talked about love to Daddy, whose eyes crinkled with tender tears and whose voice sounded funny when we children made him the most pitiful present, when we performed at school, or when he introduced us to his friends.

"To love is to live," he explained. "To be loved in return is God's gift. Think about loving, Elaine, not being loved. One day the richest kind of gift will be yours."

Oh, Daddy knew about loving.

"Upon those who love, ungenerous time bestows a thousand summers," someone once said. How true that is for me. Sunrise after sunrise over the Wasatch Range. Sunset blending with sunset behind the Oquirrhs and turning that copper Capitol dome into a fiery thing. So many summers the counting is a chore, but with memories enough to have been a thousand.

As summers came and went, each brought its own reward, each requiring something of me. My own marriage pressed young upon me because of war. Then, yet another baby to nurse, another batch of fruit to preserve, another church assignment to fill, another marriage of a beloved child. Until at last, there came one summer's end, a gathering of our family one last time before the youngest would leave for his mission.

We were at the cabin, a little place we had built ourselves in great sacrifice and joy, sharing efforts and sore thumbs with the wonderful larger family of grandparents, uncles, aunts, and cousins as close now as siblings.

We treasured this primitive place where so many summers had been spent so close to stars and wild creatures of the earth and away from the stores and shocks of civilization.

I looked at these I loved and would give my life for—grown-ups themselves now—circling the fire and quietly considering the question their father had put to us, "Well, what have you learned this summer?"

The one preparing for a mission spoke first. "My work at the restaurant put me in company with some people with a life-style far different from ours. It's been quite an eye-opener. But then I began noticing how they behaved with rude customers so free with complaints and insults. I learned that 'the soft answer turneth away wrath.' "

The young wife spoke almost with reverence. "I have learned about love. Bryant loves me anyway! And such love makes me want to please him. I'm beginning to understand something about Heavenly Father's ability to love us even when we aren't doing our best."

There had been a recent funeral for a friend of one of our girls and she had been deeply touched by the fine things said about him at the service. "I thought at the time," she said quietly, "what would they be able to say at my funeral—that I was a good dresser? Bob's death is a dramatic thrust for me to live with more purpose. That's what I've learned this summer."

And so it went, each reporting on books read and discoveries made, of skills sharpened and friendships strengthened, of scriptures memorized and principles reaffirmed, and of the wonder of bearing a child.

"How could the mother of Jesus stand to lose him?" whispered the young mother hugging her firstborn.

It was the summer of my content.

In spite of financial reverses, threatening changes, critical illness, pressures of responsibilities, lost youth, and tender nostalgia, I felt the spilling of my cup sitting in the circle of my family. This is what living is all about.

My world had broadened beyond the Hill, but my heart still found solace in the lessons of those years. Coping is contagious.

From oleander to grandmother, with my life now matching the season, I am akin to Albert Camus. "In the midst of winter I finally learned that there was in me an invincible summer."